TEN MOMENTS

MOMENTS

in Canadian History (1759-1900)

Fly The Flag High!

The Parliament Buildings in Ottawa, Canada's capital city. The Peace Tower, rising to over 302 feet (90 m) in height, is topped by the red maple leaf.

TEN
MOMENTS
IN CANADIAN HISTORY
(1759-1900)

by
Marian Ogden Sketch

INTRODUCTION
BY
BRUCE HUTCHISON

CAMPBELL'S PUBLISHING
Victoria, British Columbia, Canada

Design: Darylene van Straaten
Maps: Joan Sutton
Cover Photographs: Andrew Niemann
Printed in Canada by: Mitchell Press Ltd.

Canadian Cataloguing in Publication Data

Sketch, Marian Ogden.
    Ten Moments in Canadian History

    Includes index.
    ISBN 0-920614-06-X pa.
    ISBN 0-920614-08-6 bd.

    1. Canada - History. 2. Canada - Biography
I. Title.
FC163.S59   971   C80-091107-5
F1026.S59

CAMPBELL'S PUBLISHING
201-1150 Rockland Avenue
Victoria, B.C. V8V 3H7

ACKNOWLEDGEMENTS

**The Author and Publisher
wish to extend their thanks to the following.
Their co-operation in providing illustrations, photographs
and historical facts for**
Ten Moments in Canadian History
is certainly appreciated:

Public Archives of Canada, Ottawa
Illustrations from C. W. Jefferys *The Picture Gallery of Canadian
History* (Vols. 1-3)
Canadian Government Office of Tourism, Ottawa
Royal Canadian Mounted Police, Ottawa
Upper Canada Village - St. Lawrence Parks Commission
Niagara Parks Commission
Provincial Archives of Manitoba
Glenbow-Alberta Institute Archives
Travel Alberta
Carling O'Keefe Breweries of Canada Ltd., Calgary
Province of British Columbia Archives
Victoria City Archives
Tourism British Columbia
The Grimmer Family, Pender Island, B.C.
Andrew Niemann
Ian McKain

To my two young sons,
David and Andrew,
who did their best to delay, forestall, stymie or even eliminate
the publication of this book . . .

AUTHOR'S PREFACE

History in general has always seemed to me to be pedantic, remote and dull. From my earliest school days, memorizing dates of battles, peace treaties and other so-called significant historical events impressed me as a supremely irrelevant waste of time!

Unlike me, my sculptor husband is a history enthusiast. During years of extensive travel from Newfoundland to Vancouver Island, he became fascinated with various characters in Canadian history and visited the scenes of their exploits. His bronze figures reflect a personal story not found in most history books. The statuettes are now at various locations across Canada—most of them near where each incident depicted took place.

Since sculptors are not always literary giants, and since I was once known for my journalistic talents, we decided to collaborate on what we hope will serve as an appetizer to Canadian history.

The ten short episodes in this book are drawn from moments in the lives of an assortment of soldiers, adventurers, rebels and some seemingly ordinary people who were caught up in the building of a country.

The context is deliberately a North American one because the histories of Canada and the United States are inextricably interwoven. The location of the border, after all, was still being arbitrated on the West Coast as recently as 1868.

There has been no attempt to tell the whole story—rather it is history presented in vignettes. Nor do we lay any claim to being scholars or historians. The objective here has been to visualize—to form mental images—against a background of historical fact.

Marian Ogden Sketch

Pender Island, B.C.

TEN MOMENTS IN CANADIAN HISTORY

CONTENTS

INTRODUCTION
by
Bruce Hutchison

Through his sculpture, Ralph Sketch has developed a keen eye for history's turning points. His statuary depicts some of the men who, at decisive moments which were little understood at the time, preserved in war and peace the original ingredients of a nation yet to be. Without these men and moments no Canada would exist today.

The nation's grand, improbable experience cannot be recorded, of course, in dramatic events alone. While a few men fought on battlefields from the Plains of Abraham to the banks of the Saskatchewan, most Canadians labored peacefully to clear the wilderness and master half a continent. But political, social and economic history—the slow accretion of land, law and government—is not the focus of Ralph Sketch's chosen work. He sees instead the drama of certain events and personalizes them in bronze.

Since the events were made by men who seldom understood the subterranean forces moving beneath them, human beings are the artist's concern. And since he is himself a horseman, his heroes are invariably mounted, the animal as faithfully portrayed as the rider. The result is a cavalcade at once nostalgic, poignant and full of folk memories for all Canadians.

11

In this unique book, picturing his statues, Ralph Sketch and his wife, Marian, a skilled writer, present their heroic gallery of soldiers, statesmen and humble forgotten characters who, among others, carried the nation from sea to sea.

It was no accident, one suspects, that the artist was first attracted to the nation's adventure story by a man on horseback. Alfred, a noble gray charger, galloping from Fort George to Queenston Heights with Isaac Brock in the saddle and just two more hours of life before him, offered an irresistible theme. The reader will see how that theme is captured—the moment when Manifest Destiny's northward lunge was halted and the prospects of North America reversed.

Again, at the battle of Crysler's Farm, the sculptor has isolated another man, his mount and his moment. Then, far to the westward, two men of equal importance to the nation are seen in the Pacific Coast mountains and the gold fields of the Cariboo when British Columbia was soon to round out Confederation.

Perhaps James Douglas is the least understood figure in the annals and legendry of the continent. A factor of the Hudson's Bay Company and governor of a flimsy fort on Vancouver Island, he calmly dominated many events that settled the boundary between the United States and Canada. Douglas is shown beside the Fraser meditating there the possibility of a road from Yale, on the river, to Barkerville, capital of the gold rush. It seemed an impossible dream, but the Cariboo Road was built and British Columbia's first permanent population established.

The second mounted man, Matthew Baillie Begbie, was the only kind of judge who could have enforced the law among the prospectors, gamblers, robbers and dance-hall girls of the rush. But not until recent years has Begbie's real character been discovered and isolated from the myth of his ignorance and rash judicial judgments. Wisely, therefore, the sculptor shows him pondering some legal question, or some evidence of crime. In any case, we see Begbie, and his horse, true to life.

Then a man still less known to history appears, the builder of the Dewdney trail from the Fraser to the Kootenay region—another impossible dream that became a reality.

Ralph Sketch does not confine himself to distinguished figures. He found on Pender Island, where he lives, the footprints of a man who first settled there and survived brutal hardships unknown to his successors. In such men's unrecorded toil the nation was conceived and brought forth.

The rest of the story can be seen, and read, in the following pages. They are not intended to give a complete account but only to fix men and moments that catch the imagination. Marian Ogden Sketch's crisp, terse writing style—founded, no doubt, on massive research—explains the historical background. This partnership has produced a book providing a series of vivid glances at Canada's past, with some intimations, too, of its almost unlimited future.

Victoria, B.C.
January, 1980

Bruce Hutchison
has been a journalist for some three score years,
published many books on Canada and is now Editor Emeritus of
The Vancouver Sun.

Generale le Marquis de
MONTCALM (1712 - 1759)

Moment
Number **1:** The Plains of Abraham, Quebec
10:45 a.m. on September 13th, 1759

The guards swung open the huge portals of the Saint Louis Gate as the iron shoes of Montcalm's black horse clanged a funereal beat on the cobblestones.

From the ramparts of the fortress of Quebec, the people of New France had watched their army destroyed; now they stood back in shocked alarm. Although Montcalm was dying, he rode his black horse with dignity.

Thus the long history of the French empire in Canada had ended in a single hour. The prospects of a continent were transformed.

There were bloodstains on Montcalm's left hand and his uniform below the sash was stained dark red. The women raised their eyes to heaven – "Mon Dieu, Mon Dieu", they muttered.

His features set and his face ashen, Montcalm rode on alone. The priests crossed themselves, their lips moving.

Generale le Marquis de Montcalm

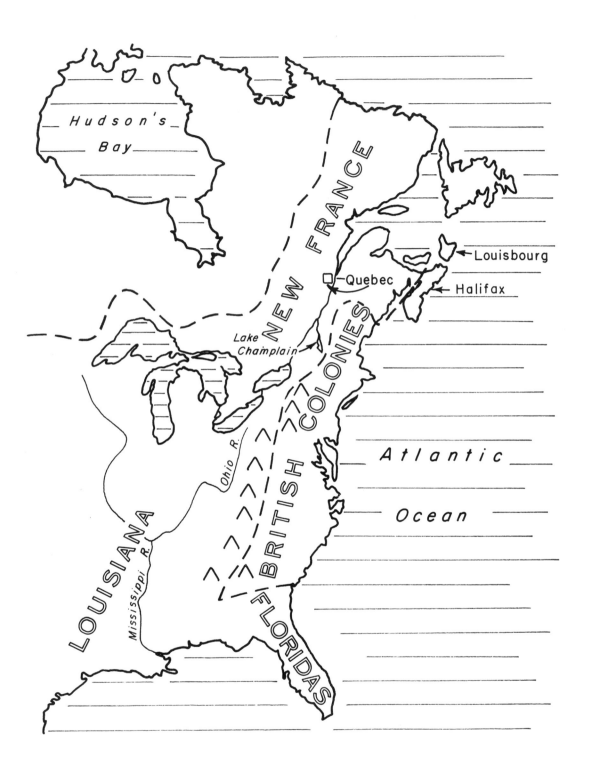

Hudson's Bay

NEW FRANCE

← Louisbourg

□ Quebec

← Halifax

Lake Champlain →

BRITISH COLONIES

Atlantic

Ocean

LOUISIANA

Ohio R.

Mississippi R.

FLORIDAS

16

*I*n the year 1759, in North America, a string of British colonies stretched along the Atlantic Seaboard from Nova Scotia to Georgia. (These colonies would not become the United States of America until after the American Revolution 17 years later; one colony, Nova Scotia, would remain British.)

The colonies were contained by a backdrop of the Appalachian Mountains to the west and a French colonial settlement on their northern flank. France ran a far-flung trading empire from Quebec with roots fanning out to the west through the Great Lakes and down the Mississippi River. With no roads, the waterways were the highways.

To the south, lay the Spanish possessions in the Floridas and Mexico. To the far west and north, spread a vast unexplored continent. It was larger than the whole of Europe and sparsely peopled by nomadic tribes of North American 'Indians'.

Plains Indians

Coureurs-de-bois

The French had no incentive to settle the interior. The Indians did the hunting for furs and then traded them to the enterprising 'coureurs-de-bois', who paddled their canoes through the Great Lakes and portaged over the short heights of land to the head waters of the Mississippi.

17

Of all the French explorers, La Vérendrye and his two sons had penetrated the farthest west in the 1730's. It is believed that they may have even seen the snow-capped peaks of the Rocky Mountains. In 1743, the two sons carried on their father's work. (At the junction of the Teton and the Missouri rivers they buried a lead plate which was found in 1913 by an American schoolgirl, Hattie May Foster.)

The brothers La Vérendrye, 1743

The somewhat decadent French court at Versailles had little interest in North American possessions except for the furs and fish they provided. Quebec was defended by two mighty fortresses. Louisbourg on Cape Breton Island guarded the approaches to the St. Lawrence River and prevented English colonial settlement from moving northward. The second fortress was the Citadel atop the massive rock cliff where Quebec City now stands.

Living on a small island, the British were far more interested in overseas possessions. They used their sailors not only for defence, but also to explore the world in search of raw materials and markets. With a heavy investment in their North American colonies, the British decided to use their sea power to oust their old rivals, the French, and grab the entire North American continent north of the Spanish possessions.

Wolfe   *Montcalm*

In 1758, the British organized a seaborne expedition with Halifax, Nova Scotia, as its base. Its objective — the French fortress at Louisbourg. After a successful seige by the British forces, Louisbourg surrendered. During the fighting, James Wolfe, a young English regular army officer, displayed courage and remarkable leadership qualities. The next year, Wolfe, promoted to the rank of General, was chosen to lead the attack against Quebec. The British were also trying to invade French territory overland from their colonies to the south. The French military commander at Quebec, General Marquis de Montcalm, led a force to meet the British at the interior forts and drove them back with bold determination.

Montcalm was a French aristocrat with professional military training which he put to good use. Nevertheless, he disliked his task as defender of the last French stronghold in North America. His position was made difficult by the ineffective Governor Vaudreuil, who frequently countermanded Montcalm's orders, and by the corrupt Administrator Bigot. "What a country, what a country," lamented Montcalm, "where knaves grow rich and honest men are ruined."

During the summer of 1759, General Wolfe, at the head of a strong British army, was transported by overpowering naval strength to blockade and cannonade the fortress of Quebec. He secured the south bank of the river but his attempts to land on the north shore downstream from the fortress were unsuccessful.

In a desperate gamble late in the season on the night of September 12th, Wolfe got his troops ashore at the base of a track that led to the top of the towering cliffs upstream from the fortress. Earlier, Montcalm had placed troops to guard the track, but Governor Vaudreuil countermanded the order, leaving only a few soldiers on guard.

Wolfe chooses his battleground and landing place

At first light on September 13th, the British army was drawn up ready for battle on the Plains of Abraham, inland from the Citadel of Quebec. Montcalm realized that if he did not dislodge the troops, his lines of communication to Montreal would be cut. After delay and further interference from Vaudreuil, Montcalm positioned his army and attacked. They were no match for the enemy. Within half an hour the battle was over — the French army was virtually destroyed and survivors were in full flight. General Wolfe died on the battlefield and Montcalm was mortally wounded.

Despite his wounds, Montcalm had himself hoisted onto his black horse and, supported by two grenadiers, rode back into the Citadel with calm and dignity. As he reached the St. Louis Gate, he ordered the grenadiers to stand aside and he rode on with his head held high. His aim was to reassure the people, arrange for the care of the wounded, and negotiate with the British.

Imagine Montcalm's state of mind at 10:45 a.m. on September 13th, 1759. He knew he would never see his wife and children or his beloved French chateau again; he knew that despite valiant fighting and brilliant defence, he had lost the last French bastion in North America. As he lay dying that night, he thanked God he would not live to see the British in charge of the fortress of Quebec.

Alfred, Isaac Brock's gray charger

General Isaac Brock's horse
ALFRED

A gray horse, Alfred, pawed the ground and whinnied, then spiraled round the hitching post. In the last few days he had carried his master, General Brock, along the Niagara riverbank as guns were placed here, defences checked there.

Now, with deafening gun blasts, smoke and shouting everywhere, his master had left him. Alfred tossed his head in irritation; he felt frightened and alone.

"They also serve who only stand and wait." Brock was already dead. Alfred's turn would come.

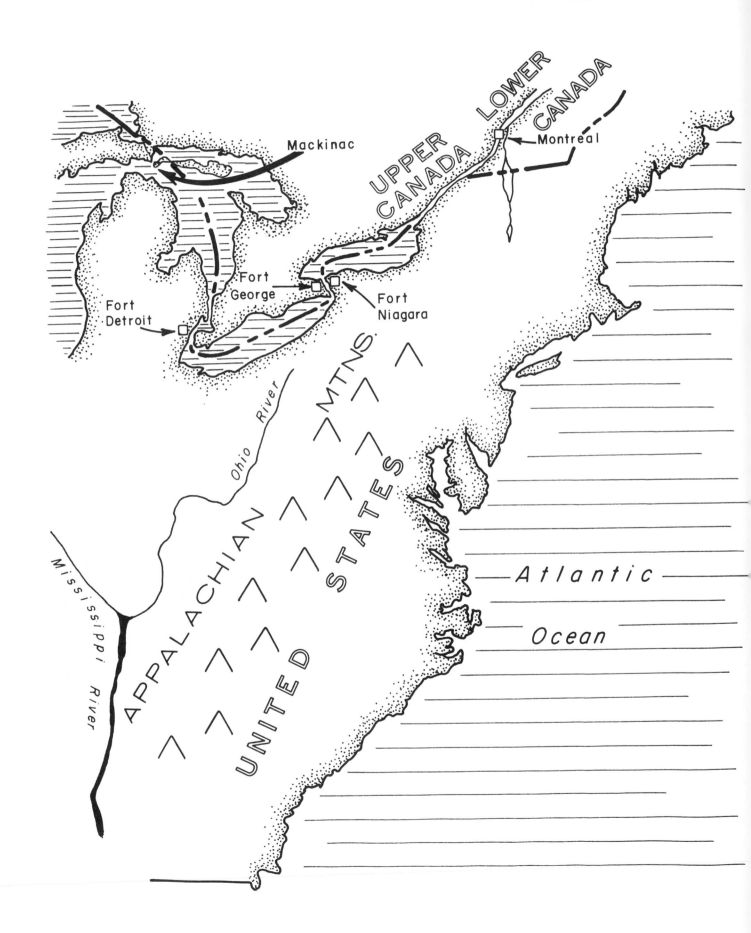

Mackinac

UPPER CANADA

LOWER CANADA

Montréal

Fort George

Fort Niagara

Fort Detroit

Ohio River

MTNS

APPALACHIAN

UNITED STATES

Mississippi River

Atlantic Ocean

$\mathcal{D}$uring the 53 years which followed the British conquest at Quebec, the balance of power in North America had changed radically. In 1776, the 13 American colonies along the Eastern Seaboard declared their independence from Britain. Quebec and Nova Scotia, despite pressures and attack from their neighbours to the south, decided not to join the revolution.

Five years of bloody battles on land and sea ended with the British surrender at Yorktown in 1781. By the terms of peace, a border was set up between the newly-established United States of America and the remaining British colonies to the north.

Indians trading furs, 1785

The map shows the beginnings of a border running from east to west, leaving the watershed of the St. Lawrence River and the northern half of the Great Lakes in the 'Canadas' — Upper Canada on the upper reaches of the St. Lawrence and Lower Canada downstream. While the destiny of North America was being determined on the east coast, the Hudson's Bay Company, from its northern base, was pushing its fur trading routes to the west and south. Rival fur traders from Montreal, the North West Company, competed aggressively by setting up a chain of forts reaching out to even beyond the Rocky Mountains.

One of the North West Company's young traders and adventurers, Alexander Mackenzie, was heartbroken when, after all his hardships, he discovered that the river he had followed (which now bears his name) flowed into the Arctic Ocean and not into the Pacific. Four years later, he became the first white man to cross the continent. On reaching the Pacific at Bella Coola, Mackenzie painted a poignant message on a slab of rock — 'Alexander Mackenzie from Canada, by land, the twenty-second of July, one thousand seven hundred and ninety-three. Lat 52 20 48 N.'

The ideals of the American Revolution — democratic government and the concept that all men are created equal — helped inspire a revolution in France a few years later. But the French battle cry — "Liberté, Egalité, Fraternité" — was soon pushed aside when a Corsican military genius, Napoleon Bonaparte, took advantage of the near-anarchy that followed the revolution to establish a military dictatorship. Napoleon's dream was to conquer — first Europe, then the world.

Back in North America, U.S. President Thomas Jefferson was busy pursuing his own vision of a continental empire. After Napoleon's ambitious plans of world conquest faltered, following a slave revolt on the French West Indian island of Haiti, the Americans were able to conclude purchase of the Louisiana territory from France.

To explore the new territory and find a suitable route to Oregon, Jefferson dispatched an expedition led by Lewis and Clark. They reached the Pacific at the mouth of the Columbia River in 1805.

American migration and settlement were pushing westward through the Appalachian mountain passes and down the Ohio River. Trouble erupted as the Indians saw their ancient hunting grounds threatened. Some of the Indians who raided and butchered in the new American settlements operated from the shelter of British territory to the north. Among them was a warrior who was to play an important part in the coming war. His name was Tecumseh, the chief of the Shawnee Indians.

Brock and Tecumseh meet, 1812

In 1812, the British were again at war with France, trying desperately to defend their islands from Napoleon's grand army at Boulogne. One effect of the British naval blockade of Europe was to interfere with American ships attempting to trade with France. When President Madison, Jefferson's successor, declared war on Britain in June, 1812, he gave as his reason the attacks on U.S. shipping and the suspected tacit approval by the British of the western Indian raids.

But the ultimate U.S. objective, as put forward by at least some of its political leaders, was much more sweeping than any of these relatively petty grievances. The war hawk group in Congress, led by Henry Clay of Kentucky, believed that, with Britain so preoccupied in Europe, the timing was ideal to move against Canada. The moment had come to kick the British right out of North America, just as Britain had done to France. Clay and his supporters also believed, probably quite genuinely, that the people of Canada would welcome an opportunity to be liberated from the British yoke. Invading Canada, in short, would be a pushover.

To Britain, struggling for survival, the war in North America was a side-show and a nuisance. The Canadian settlers, however, were justifiably shocked and alarmed. At the time, the total population of the Canadas was less that 500,000 people, compared with almost eight million Americans.

Most of the English-speaking Canadians had come as British Loyalists from the United States after the American Revolution. While the majority settled in Nova Scotia, Prince Edward Island and Lower Canada, many took up land in Upper Canada along the St. Lawrence River and on the north shore of Lake Ontario. In view of the overwhelming odds against them, should the U.S. invade, it seemed doubtful that these new settlers would flock to the colours in support of the tiny British regular army.

General Isaac Brock, military commander of Upper Canada, was a tall blond bachelor who was as bold as his training had been thorough. He quickly realized that a resounding victory against the Americans would give the Canadians confidence that they could in fact defend their new homeland.

Rather than sit in his headquarters at Fort George, where he was defending the Niagara frontier, Brock took the bull by the horns. With the aid of Indian warriors led by Tecumseh, he pulled off two spectacular swoops. He first sent a force to seize the U.S. stronghold on the island of Mackinac, then grabbed Fort Detroit—thus, in effect, taking a surrender of the entire American northwest.

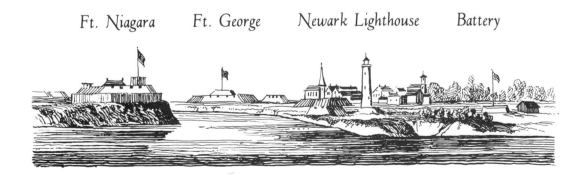

Ft. Niagara   Ft. George   Newark Lighthouse   Battery

Hustling his small army back to the Niagara River, Brock was thankful that the Americans had not decided to cross above or below the great falls at a time when there was nothing to defend his fort but a corporal's guard—a mere handful of soldiers! Brock's force included a few hundred British regulars—the rest were Canadian militia and Indians—1,000 in all. The Americans massed 10,000 troops at Lewiston across from Queenston and the escarpment that rises above it.

Early on the morning of October 13th, 1812, Brock was awakened by the terrifying sounds of a heavy bombardment from the American shore of the Niagara River. He assumed that the expected invasion was on, but he did not know whether the crossing would be aimed at Fort George or nearer the falls at the Heights above Queenston, opposite the American camp.

Brock's ride to Queenston Heights, Ontario

Brock had to find out. He sent for his gray horse, Alfred, who was well known by sight on both sides of the river, and galloped seven miles through the cold first light to the village of Queenston. On the way he became convinced that the American objective was the Heights of the escarpment; he sent word back to General Shaeffe at the fort to bring up all the troops.

By the time Brock reached Queenston, the Americans were crossing the river in large numbers. Soon after nine o'clock on that fateful morning, Alfred was tethered to a hitching post in the village — sweating, heaving and fretting for his master. About the same time, Brock was leading a charge on foot in an attempt to regain a gun which had been captured halfway up the Heights. During the fighting, Brock was killed.

Alfred's memorial at Queenston Heights, Ontario

Later in the day, Brock's aide-de-camp, Colonel John Macdonnell, another tall man in scarlet coat and white breeches, rode Alfred hoping to convey the impression that the General was still alive. As he led another attack on the American positions, Macdonnell was fatally wounded and Alfred was shot dead beneath him. These seemingly unsuccessful charges prevented the Americans from entrenching their positions; meanwhile, the main body of British and Canadian troops was on the way up to the front.

The charges had another more powerful effect. Less than a quarter of the American force, which was commanded by General Van Renssalaer, had crossed the river to actually engage in the fighting. The rest, nearly all citizen soldiers who were not entirely convinced that they should be at war except as liberators, stood on the opposite bank watching the terrible hostility and furious opposition. As a result, when it was their turn to embark, many refused.

After the main body of British troops led by General Shaeffe arrived from Fort George in the early afternoon, the disillusioned Americans were beaten back across the river. They left behind 1,000 prisoners — equal to the total of Brock's forces! Canada had been saved, at least for the time being.

A fine memorial now stands on the Queenston Heights to remind us of General Brock and his brave men. Remember also a gray horse, tethered and fretting for a master he would never see after 9:45 a.m. on October 13th, 1812.

Lt. Colonel Joseph
MORRISON (1783 - 1826)

Moment Number **3:** Crysler's Farm, Ontario
4:30 p.m. on November 11th, 1813

The smoke of battle, the blinding gun flashes and the rifle volleys terrified his horse, but Morrison was as much at home on a plunging horse as a sea captain on his bridge.

Late in the day as the American lines faltered, Morrison ordered the 49th Regiment to attack the enemy guns. Suddenly, he saw a squadron of American cavalry forming up to charge the British right flank: "Check the 49th — stop that damned cavalry!"

Here was a moment — Canada was saved by the skin of her teeth.

Lt. Colonel Joseph Morrison
The desperate battle in which he fought, is vividly depicted in the mural at
Crysler's Farm Battle Memorial Building, near Morrisburg, Ontario

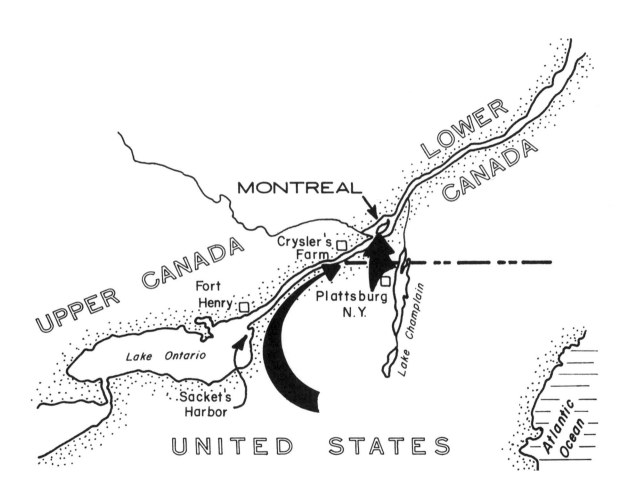

LOWER CANADA

MONTREAL

Crysler's Farm

UPPER CANADA

Fort Henry

Plattsburg N.Y.

Lake Champlain

Lake Ontario

Sacket's Harbor

UNITED STATES

Atlantic Ocean

$\mathcal{B}$rock's victory at the Niagara frontier saved Canada in the initial battles of the War of 1812, but she remained in desperate peril of invasion by the United States for two more years.

Battles, mostly fought on Canadian soil, were won and lost by both sides. American Commodore Oliver Perry, commanding the U.S. Navy, outsailed and outgunned the British fleet on Lake Erie, gaining virtual control of the Great Lakes west of Lake Ontario. Canada, however, hung on to the strategic island of Mackinac, where Lakes Huron, Michigan and Superior come together. The warm coats made out of colourful Hudson's Bay blankets for the brave, isolated defenders became known as Mackinaws — the word has lived on.

When either Canada or Canadian soil is mentioned, it should be remembered that Confederation of the British colonies which created Canada was not to come into being for another 55 years. So, in 1812/1813, the colonies were still administered, except for detail, from London. The war, therefore, was between the Americans and the British. As it progressed, however, more and more settlers, fur trappers and farmers joined the militia units or provided replacements among the regular British units. A better trained and growing army of defenders was in the making.

Laura Secord
She gave the cow a swift kick and ran after it into the woods

Laura Secord (1775 - 1868)

*I*n the spring of 1813, the Americans captured Fort George and occupied the Canadian shore of the Niagara River, including the village of Queenston. The most forward post still held by the British on the Niagara peninsula was the strategic crossroads at Beaver Dams, near the present city of St. Catharines. There, Lieutenant James Fitzgibbon commanded 30 regular British soldiers and a large detachment of Indians.

The Americans ordered a force of almost 700 men to seize the Beaver Dams outpost. A surprise attack shortly before dawn was planned for June 23rd, 1813, but was later postponed for 24 hours. A few days before the operation, some American soldiers were in the home of James Secord, a Canadian soldier who had been seriously wounded the previous fall in Brock's battle at Queenston Heights. The soldiers, billeted in the home, carelessly chatted about the battle plans and were overheard by Mrs. Laura Secord. Laura had several young children as well as her wounded husband to care for. Nevertheless, she decided she must try to warn the outpost at Beaver Dams of the impending attack. The initial problem was to get by the American sentries.

Part of her normal daily routine was to rise early and go out to the meadow to milk their cow. On the morning of June 22nd, she pretended she couldn't catch the docile animal. Giving it a swift kick, she ran after the cow as it disappeared into the woods. To the watching sentries, it all seemed harmless enough. What they didn't know was that Laura Secord would spend that hot sultry day fighting her way through 20 miles of dense forest—alone in a no-man's land patrolled by trigger-happy Indian scouts. Late in the evening, she finally staggered into the British outpost, her clothes in shreds, and was escorted to Fitzgibbon's headquarters in the De Cou farmhouse.

Laura Secord tells her story to Fitzgibbon, 1813

When the attack came on the night of June 24th, the British were ready. An Indian ambush wrought havoc on the U.S. troops in the darkness and, soon afterwards, a badly mauled American column surrendered.

The story has become a classic Canadian legend—the sort of legend which helps to build the character of a nation. Unfortunately, the Laura Secord story has a sad ending. After her husband died and his small veteran's pension was clipped off, Laura applied to the Upper Canada government for a pension of her own. Her application became a political issue, and, although James Fitzgibbon signed two certificates verifying the heroic incident, Laura Secord never got her pension.

This brave woman did, however, become the symbol of countless Canadian women who kept their homes together, tended the wounded, and defied the invading enemy, while their men were away fighting.

Early in 1813, the Americans decided to shift their emphasis away from Upper Canada—to the east and the all-important supply centre of Montreal. This much larger invasion was to be in the form of a pincer movement.

U.S. General Wade Hampton, with 7,000 troops based in Plattsburg, New York, was to move north by way of the Chateauguay Valley. His approach on Montreal was to be carefully timed to coincide with a force of 8,000 men led by General James Wilkinson which was to head down the St. Lawrence River from Lake Ontario. Once the jaws of the pincer clamped tight on Montreal, any possibility of further supplies or military help from Britain would be blocked.

de Salaberry

Wilkinson

During the summer of 1813, the corrupt, overweight, liquor-swilling Wilkinson concentrated his force at Sacket's Harbor on the American shore of Lake Ontario. Initially, he planned to destroy Fort Henry at Kingston before proceeding unmolested down river.

As summer slipped into fall, the maples took on their flaming reds and golds. In view of the lateness of the season, it was decided to by-pass Fort Henry, well-defended by the British behind solid fortifications.

By early November, with the icy blasts of the northern winter already blowing, the long-delayed invasion was underway at last. Wilkinson's army, in ships and barges, slipped through the Thousand Islands and made its way by stages down the St. Lawrence. Wade Hampton's force was also on the move. Word of these massive troop movements soon reached Fort Henry. The citizens of Kingston were relieved that they were to be spared, although they were fully aware of the consequences if the Americans captured both banks of the river at Montreal.

Young Lt. Colonel Joseph Morrison, who had sound British army training but limited experience of command in battle, was chosen to lead the British and Canadian forces from Kingston. His little army was made up of British regulars, stoic Scottish highlanders, militia and a few naval gunners—900 in all.

British Sergeant

As soon as the Americans started down river, Morrison carried out his prearranged plan. Loaded on gunboats and barges, his men shadowed the enemy. When the American forces landed on the Canadian bank above the rapids at Long Sault, Morrison put his troops ashore just upstream, having selected the open fields of John Crysler's farm as his battlefield. His men spent the icy wet night of November 10th camped around the farm buildings.

British General

The night before the inevitable battle, Morrison gave orders to his regimental commanders with outward confidence. He calmly walked his camp—checking the men on watch here, offering a word of encouragement there—full of dreadful trepidation.

Early the next morning, skirmishers were sent forward to bait the enemy onto the battlefield. In the meantime, Morrison formed up his troops for a full-fledged engagement in open country. This suited the British soldiers' training in formation fighting but was unwelcome to the Americans, who displayed their best qualities in bush fighting.

U.S. General Boyd, in charge of Wilkinson's rear guard, had 4,000 troops under his command including strong artillery and a squadron of cavalry. It was Boyd's job to remove the menace of Morrison's troops so that the main body of Wilkinson's army could proceed on its way to Montreal. The Americans put in large-scale, repeated attacks, but the British line held firm, firing in disciplined volleys.

The critical point of the battle came as the afternoon light was beginning to fade. With his aide-de-camp and two or three gallopers, Morrison sat astride a fretting horse on a hilltop from which he could view the whole battle scene. Suddenly, he saw a squadron of American cavalry forming up, getting ready to charge along the River Road. Morrison realized that the Americans intended to turn his right flank and get in behind his line of battle. They had to be stopped, or all might be lost. Imagine Morrison's instant reaction—his heart pounding, he shouted to his aide above the roar and clash of guns, "Stop that damned cavalry!" It was 4:30 p.m. on November 11th, 1813.

The Battle of Crysler's Farm, 1813

The U.S. troopers advanced bravely, but by that time Morrison's flank companies were ready. There were many empty saddles before the American cavalry reached the British line. The charge was successfully repulsed.

41

The British and Canadians were supported by the cannon on their ships anchored in the river; in the resulting havoc, the American lines broke and retreated. During the night, Wilkinson's entire army crossed back to the American shore. By that time, word had reached Wilkinson that Wade Hampton's troops had been stopped dead on the Chateauguay River by a determined force under the intrepid French-Canadian, Colonel Charles de Salaberry.

Because of the lateness in the year, and to some extent Wilkinson's weak leadership, the whole campaign against Montreal was abandoned. More unsuccessful attempts at invasion were made during the following summer, but when hostilities ceased the Americans held no Canadian soil. The British had captured Fort Niagara and hung on to the American shore of the Niagara River. The Royal Navy secured and held one-third of the coast of Maine as far south as Penobscot Bay.

Early in 1814, American delegates met with the British at Ghent in Belgium to negotiate terms of peace. Included among the delegates, ironically enough, was Congressman Henry Clay of Kentucky who had led his country into a declaration of war by a narrow margin of votes. The British negotiators at the peace talks were in a relatively strong position. The menace of Napoleon had been temporarily removed by his exile to the island of Elba, so the British were free to divert units of their army and navy to North America.

The terms of peace, finally agreed upon on Christmas Eve, 1814, reflected none of the objectives for which the United States had gone to war—the sorry affair ended with the re-establishment of the original border. While Canadians felt the British had been far too generous in giving up their hard-won gains, the principal objective, of course, was to secure a long-term peace.

As the delegates were discussing peace terms and before news of the agreement reached the other side of the Atlantic, the British, perhaps ill-advisedly, put in a series of punitive raids on the Atlantic Seaboard. They burned the Capitol and the White House in Washington. They attacked Baltimore ineffectively and were repulsed when they attempted to raid New Orleans.

In that there were victories on both sides, the self-respect of each warring nation had been maintained. One consequence of the war may have been an awareness on the part of the Americans that the citizens of the Canadas were not ready to embrace democratic republicanism —a concept then about as suspect as communism is today in the Western world.

A more memorable by-product for the United States was that a young American lawyer named Francis Scott Key, on a mission to obtain the exchange of an American prisoner, was detained aboard a British man-of-war that was bombarding Fort McHenry at Baltimore. Key watched the terrible shelling and mortar fire through the long anxious night. The next morning, when he saw that the Stars and Stripes were still flying over the fort, he wrote a poem. Its opening words were: 'Oh, say can you see, by the dawn's early light . . .'

For the people of the Canadas, the aftermath of the war was lasting indeed. Their homes, their farms and their towns had been sacked, and many a brave son was mourned. A feeling of bitterness and apprehension toward Americans endured for generations. The apprehension lingers on today, although its origin may have been forgotten.

In Upper Canada, where the settlements were not much more than 30 years old, a new sense of pride and nationhood emerged as the colony discovered, to its amazement, that it could withstand heavy odds. Both Upper and Lower Canada acquired a new confidence in each other, despite differences in their history and ethnic origins.

For Lt. Colonel Morrison, the end of the war brought promotion and other campaigns on distant battlefields. He died as a result of illness in 1826 on a troopship taking him back to England. "It is a tale of old, far-off, unhappy things, and battles long ago."

Most of the Crysler's Farm fields were flooded over when the St. Lawrence Seaway was built in 1959. On part of the land that remains along the new shoreline near Morrisburg, Ontario, an attractive long, low stone building is now the Crysler's Farm Battle Memorial Building. One wall of the darkened central hall is covered with a flood-lit mural. It dramatically illustrates the turning point in that desperate battle.

What must have been Joseph Morrison's finest hour—and what was certainly a crucial moment for Canada—came at 4:30 p.m. on November 11th, 1813.

William Lyon
MACKENZIE (1795 - 1861)

Moment Number **4:** On the road to Dundas, Ontario
7:00 p.m. on December 7th, 1837

Fearing for his life, William Lyon Mackenzie booted his flying horse on into the dark night. Before his rebellion, Mackenzie had defied the Legislative Assembly in Upper Canada, shouted for democratic government and printed condemnation of the status quo in his newspaper.

But Mackenzie's rebellion had collapsed and his supporters were scattered; he was haunted by the hangman.

William Lyon Mackenzie flees in the night.
(Plaster stage for the bronze statuette)

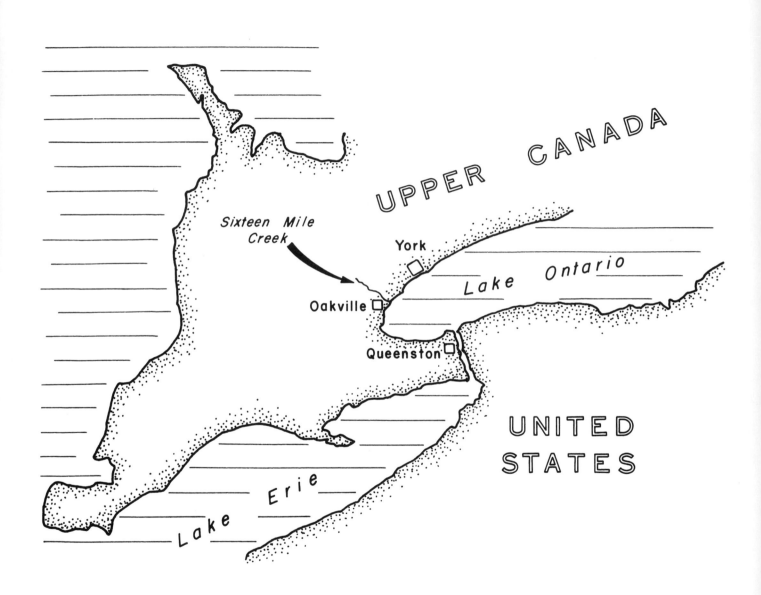

UPPER CANADA

Sixteen Mile
Creek

York

Lake Ontario

Oakville

Queenston

UNITED
STATES

Lake Erie

It was bitterly cold and dark on the night of December 7th, 1837. A small man was crouched in the saddle, galloping down the old Dundas Road away from Toronto, toward the safety of the American border. In desperation, he urged his horse on, looking back anxiously over his shoulder every few minutes for pursuers. The next day on the steep banks of the Sixteen Mile Creek north of Oakville, he was nearly caught. But the fiery rebel managed, through subterfuge and guile, to cross into the United States a few days later. There he began many years of exile from the Canada he tried so vociferously to change.

On board an immigrant ship in the 1830's

This fugitive—William Lyon Mackenzie—had been one of many immigrants from the British Isles who flooded into Upper and Lower Canada during the 20 years of peace which followed the War of 1812. Mackenzie was born in Scotland. His experiences there made him yearn for a new way of life—he had an abiding hatred for the privileged and a society in which, as Winston Churchill said much later, "life was for the few—and for the very few!"

The diminutive Scot was joined in Canada by his devoted mother, his illegitimate son, James, and a prospective young bride. They settled in the village of Queenston on the Niagara River—a few years previously the site of General Brock's valiant stand against the Americans.

Mackenzie started a weekly newspaper and used it as a voice to call for representative government. Greatly influenced by the democratic ideals of the American Revolution, he made many friends across the border and was a champion of the U.S. form of government over the British colonial system.

The time was ripe for protest. In both Upper and Lower Canada, for quite different reasons, there were growing rumblings of discontent. The colonies had not been granted the freedoms already claimed in Britain, where cabinet ministers were elected by the people. Although there was an elected assembly in Upper Canada, the real power rested with the Lieutenant-Governor and his appointed Legislative Council.

In Upper Canada, the colonial government was run by a theatrical, rather dim-witted Lieutenant-Governor—Sir Francis Bond Head. He and the all-important council represented not the people but an entrenched 'Family Compact'—a handful of wealthy influential families. The council was also dominated by the powerful Church of England— itself the recipient of massive land grants.

Drawn to the centre of activity, William Lyon Mackenzie moved his family and his newspaper to Toronto—known colloquially as Muddy York. Elected as a member of the Legislative Assembly, Mackenzie soon became the spokesman for the most radical of the Reform groups. Other more moderate Reformers, led by such men as Robert Baldwin and Egerton Ryerson, sought to replace the Legislative Council with a Cabinet drawn from elected members of the Assembly—on the pattern of the British Parliament. But for Mackenzie and his followers, nothing short of an American-style government and a complete break with the past would do.

Mackenzie's slight build was topped by a large, high-browed head on which he wore a flaming red wig—somehow symbolic of his hot temper. The restive, stubborn Scot, bursting to express his new-found freedom, was given to fiery outbursts against the establishment. These were often without any well thought out plan of alternative action.

Papineau

Meanwhile, in Lower Canada, a very different voice of protest was being heard in a much more elegant manner. Louis-Joseph Papineau was the highly educated spokesman for the French seigniorial system, which could see its power and traditions being eroded in favour of the British colonial government. Papineau lived in baronial splendour on his estate, the Seigniory of Montebello (now a plush resort hotel) on the Ottawa River.

The two protestors—Mackenzie and Papineau—while widely divergent in temperament and in their reasons for discontent, had a common enemy in the British colonial establishment. They realized that if they led armed rebellions in both colonies simultaneously, the British troops would be hard put to cope with both uprisings at the same time.

Compounding this atmosphere of political unrest, an economic depression had set in during the 1830's. Men were out of work and farmers were getting poor prices for their crops. In their frustration, people blamed governments they could not control. Mass meetings, unwisely ignored by the government, led to secret rendezvous and loosely-organized planning for armed rebellion.

In the late fall of 1837, trouble broke out in Lower Canada. Small but savage uprisings, first at St. Denis and then at St. Eustache, became violent clashes with British redcoats. Sir Francis Bond Head, in dramatic rashness, sent all his troops to Lower Canada, leaving their City Hall armoury in Toronto virtually unguarded.

This was the signal to Mackenzie. Out went word to his followers to rally at Montgomery's Tavern on Upper Yonge Street, three miles north of the city. The rebels were to be armed with guns and pitchforks ready for action. No provision was made for accommodation or the feeding of some hundreds of men. It was snowing on December 4th and the only chance of success lay in immediate bold action—to move on the city and seize the armoury.

But Mackenzie ranted, raved and hesitated. A half-hearted attempt was made at a sally. Some raids and more hesitation occupied the next two days. Then Bond Head bestirred himself. He called up militia units and by noon on December 7th, a military show of strength marched up Yonge Street. Bond Head's force fired a few rounds at the half-starved,

Rebels marching down Yonge Street to attack Toronto, 1837

disheartened rebels and one artillery shell crashed into Montgomery's Tavern. The rebels turned and fled.

One of the first to swing into the saddle was Mackenzie, who galloped west toward the U.S. border. He had already arranged for his family to meet him in the United States, should things go wrong. Although Mackenzie escaped arrest, many of his fellow rebels were caught and some were hanged.

These apparently unsuccessful uprisings speeded the day of responsible representative government in Canada. The message which finally reached London was loud and clear—immediate action was needed to avoid a repeat performance of the tragic American Revolution of some 60 years earlier.

In 1838, the Earl of Durham was sent from England by the British government to investigate the causes of Canadian unrest. Arriving in Quebec, this resplendent aristocrat rode a white horse from his ship to the

Chateau St. Louis. Nine months later, the Durham Report was presented to the British Parliament. This report resulted eventually in truly representative governments in both Upper and Lower Canada under a governor appointed by the Crown.

As for William Lyon Mackenzie, after many years in exile, he was pardoned in 1849 and returned to Toronto. He lived in a house on Bond Street, bought for him by his old supporters. His daughter, Isabel, who had suffered from the years of exile and the public criticism of her notorious father, married John King after their return to Canada. She named her son William Lyon Mackenzie King and brought him up with one aim in mind—to vindicate her father's name. Isabel's son was to become one of Canada's most celebrated prime ministers.

William Lyon Mackenzie, as he fled on that dark night on December 7th, 1837, must have felt like a *fugitive from injustice*. This same rebellious spirit and unwillingness to endure oppression lives on in Canada today.

Governor James Douglas

Governor James
DOUGLAS (1803 - 1877)

Moment
Number **5:** Fraser Canyon, British Columbia
Noon on May 29th, 1861

As Governor Douglas' horse drank, the pounding white water cascading over the falls proclaimed the power of nature. The shadows of the overhanging mountains crowded in. Could mere man turn a cliff-hanging canyon trail into a wagon road?

Somewhere, somehow, a road from the coast had to reach the gold fields in the interior—or British Columbia might be lost. 'A capital good claret' helped to find the solution.

Cariboo Country

BRITISH COLUMBIA

Fraser River

Columbia River

Lillooet →

Lake Harrison

Yale

Vancouver's Island

Victoria

San Juan Island

Pacific

Ocean

Fort Vancouver

UNITED STATES

$\mathscr{I}$t was noon on a sunny, spring day. A tall commanding figure with a strong square jaw stopped to water his horse below a waterfall that tumbled down the towering cliffs of the Fraser Canyon, a few miles north of the village of Yale. He had just passed a little kiosk run by two Frenchmen where he planned to have lunch; but first, like any good traveller of his day, he saw to his horse before he looked after himself. As the horse sucked in the fresh cool water, pawing at the pounding stream, many conflicting thoughts were going through the mind of Governor James Douglas—so often and so rightly referred to as the Father of British Columbia.

Early prospectors were discovering extremely large quantities of gold in the streams flowing into the Fraser River hundreds of miles north in the Cariboo country. The California gold rush was losing its lustre, and thousands upon thousands of gold seekers, mostly from the United States, were flocking to British Columbia.

Early Victoria

Douglas was Governor of the tiny British colony centred around Fort Victoria on Vancouver's Island (later Vancouver Island). His problem was to select the most practical route for a wagon road to the gold fields. There were advocates of the hazardous Fraser Canyon route, but others favoured the partially-waterborne route across Lake Harrison and from there through a series of lakes and portages to rejoin the Fraser near Lillooet.

Douglas knew that, without adequate communication to the coast, those supplying goods to the gold fields and bringing out the gold would follow existing north-south valley routes, channeling the riches into the U.S. A new road was imperative to keep the wealth within British Columbia. More serious still, if he could not keep law and order among all those gun-toting, claim-jumping, quick-money adventurers, the U.S. might well have an excuse for moving in its cavalry to protect the rights of American citizens.

Such a move, as Douglas was well aware, would have fitted in admirably with U.S. aspirations. Ever since the build-up of settlement in the Oregon territory and when the purchase of Alaska from the Russians had become a likelihood, the American government had been eyeing the land in between, with the idea of controlling the entire Pacific coast.

So, a decision as to the best route for the road to the Cariboo gold fields had to be made. There was no time to wait for the blessing of the Colonial Office in London, which was not known for making split-second decisions. In any event, it took at least six weeks for a letter to reach England by the long sea route.

Knowing all this, Douglas had arranged to borrow money for building the road. He was already out on a limb and a mistake in the selection of the route would be disastrous to his career and to British interests.

There was much to trouble the governor as he led his horse back to the kiosk hitching post. His diary speaks of the magnificence of the scenery, the beauty of the spring flowers and the surprisingly good lunch, including "a capital good claret!" In a mellow mood, Douglas began to think that Colonel Moody and his Royal Engineers could, in fact, widen the pack horse trail. The narrow trail had, in places, been cut into the sheer rock cliffs. Such a continuous road would eliminate laborious trans-shipments by water. The cheering effect of the claret almost certainly influenced the road pattern we see in British Columbia today.

Sir James Douglas

Douglas was born in 1803 in British Guiana where his father, a Scottish businessman, owned plantations. His mother was a Creole. Young Douglas, schooled in Scotland, came to Canada to join the North West Company and, incidentally, to escape the smugness of Scottish society. Following the merger between the North West Company and the Hudson's Bay Company, he became second man to the famed Doctor McLaughlin, Chief Factor at Fort Vancouver on the Columbia River. (Fort Vancouver was close to where the city of Portland, Oregon, stands today.)

In 1842, American settlers were flooding into the Oregon territory. As the population built up and the Indians departed, McLaughlin realized that the Hudson's Bay Company, with its emphasis on fur trading, would have to retreat. He sent Douglas to find a new west coast headquarters. It was to be north of the 49th parallel or somewhere offshore that could easily be defended.

Douglas was disappointed at this decision. He had long believed that the border should follow the Columbia River south to the sea, leaving to Britain the major part of the present State of Washington. Nevertheless, he selected a spot on the southern tip of Vancouver's Island where there were two good harbours. It was there that Douglas built Fort Victoria in 1843. As the population slowly grew around the fort, Vancouver Island became a colony and Douglas was appointed its Governor, in addition to his duties with the Hudson's Bay Company.

The earlier retreat from the Oregon territory was an experience Douglas was never to forget—it reinforced his determination to avoid further encroachment by the Americans. In the 1860's, however, Douglas had to accept another retreat.

Victoria lay offshore some distance south of the 49th parallel. The Treaty of Washington, signed in 1846 between Britain and the United States, stated that after the 49th parallel reached the Pacific, the border would turn south and follow the centre of navigation between the mainland and Vancouver Island. It would then run westward through the Juan de Fuca Strait out to the Pacific. The exact location of the boundary had not been specified.

Of the many larger islands in the Straits, the closest to Fort Victoria was San Juan Island—peopled by both British settlers and Americans. The main trading post was run by the Hudson's Bay Company. The San Juan Islanders had the best of both worlds. When a tax collector arrived from Victoria, they took the attitude that they were Americans; but when an American tax man landed, they said they were British subjects.

Despite this outward display of solidarity, feelings between British and American residents began to show signs of strain. A climax of sorts was reached when a pig belonging to the manager of the Hudson's Bay store strayed onto an American farmer's land and proceeded to uproot his potatoes. The irate American shot the pig—a fairly high-handed thing to do as the manager of the Hudson's Bay Company was the uncrowned king of the island!

Governor Douglas was hopping mad—it was high time to put a stop to this nonsense. The British Navy had a base at Esquimalt Harbour near Victoria and Douglas dispatched a gunboat to settle the whole affair. The American settlers screamed for help; soon an American gunboat arrived and put troops ashore. Douglas retaliated by also landing troops. For a while, the situation, in what became know as the Pig War, seemed menacing.

Fortunately, the commanders of the two groups of professional soldiers were not so emotionally involved. They decided amicably, over a cup of tea, to make their encampments at opposite ends of the island. To relieve the boredom, they entertained at joint parties.

Months went by. Communications were exchanged between London and Washington. Finally it was decided that the fate of San Juan Island should be submitted to Kaiser Wilhelm of Germany for arbitration. After listening to both sides and poring over charts of the area, Kaiser Bill ponderously announced, in 1868, that San Juan Island belonged to the Americans.

It was only then that the long struggle for the border was finally settled. So began an era of good neighbours living peacefully on both sides of the longest undefended border in the world.

Ironically, having survived the rigours of the Pig War, George Edward Pickett, the young commander of the American force on San Juan Island, went east to fight with the Southern army in the American Civil War. He was destined to lead Pickett's Charge, the last desperate and tragic thrust at Cemetery Ridge in the Battle of Gettysburg.

Governor Douglas, embittered by the Kaiser's decision, grew more and more autocratic and authoritarian. Only after repeated pressures from the people of his colony and from the Colonial Office in London did he reluctantly agree to the beginnings of representative government. Douglas was never quite sold on the idea of 'government of the people, by the people'.

In the early days, an autocratic hand was needed to lay the foundations of British Columbia. During the gold rush crisis, Douglas had realized that strict law enforcement was essential. He asked the Colonial Office to send him a young judge who possessed the moral and physical strength to condemn a criminal to be hanged and then, if necessary, carry out the sentence himself.

Judge Matthew Baillie Begbie was sent and he was the man for a new country. Begbie travelled hundreds of miles, mostly on horseback. Then, dressed in wig and gown, he held court in log cabins or as he sat on his horse in the corner of a field. An imposing figure wherever he went, Begbie shared Douglas' belief in the need for a stern form of justice. Together they ruled the huge mainland territory from Victoria.

After Douglas retired, he lived aloof in his mansion on James Bay, close to where the Provincial Parliament Buildings overlook Victoria's Inner Harbour. At a retirement dinner given for him in New Westminster, Douglas, still conscious of past criticisms of his dictatorial manner, said, in a masterpiece of understatement, "I hope it will be thought that I have done my duty." (It should be remembered that the present City of Vancouver did not come into existence until after the Canadian Pacific

Railway was built. The mainland commercial centre was then New Westminster.)

Judge Matthew Baillie Begbie

James Douglas had created and preserved British Columbia, its very name symbolic of the retreat from the mouth of the Columbia River. With the promise of the Canadian Pacific Railway, the colony came into Canadian Confederation, fulfilling Sir John A. Macdonald's dream of a nation from Atlantic to Pacific.

In creating this westernmost province, Governor Douglas had been faced with many difficult decisions. Perhaps the boldest and most far-reaching was the one he pondered as he watered his horse where the Five Mile Creek flows into the Fraser River, at noon on May 29th, 1861.

The Cariboo Road to the gold fields of British Columbia. Miners are going in and the coach coming out with gold is guarded by armed men. Built by the Royal Engineers, the Cariboo Road took three years to complete. It was 18 feet wide and almost 500 miles long; one of the finest roads ever built.

Edgar
DEWDNEY (1835 - 1916)

Moment
Number **6:** Eholt Summit, British Columbia
11:00 a.m. on May 4th, 1865

It had been a long slow climb eastward out of the valley. The animals of Edgar Dewdney's pack train heaved and panted their way to the Eholt Summit.

As Dewdney pulled up his tired horse, the pack mule bumped him from behind. Shading his eyes from the bright sunlight, the young surveyor from England gazed out on a vista of endless ranges of towering mountains.

Suddenly, the immensity of his assignment hit him. Could he, in one summer, find a way and build a trail through these hundreds of miles of uncharted wilderness? What had he taken on? What was he doing here?

Edgar Dewdney

In terms of North America, 1865 stands out as the year in which the terrible American Civil War ended. At a little crossroads at Appomattox Court House in Virginia, the two military commanders, General Robert E. Lee for the South and General Ulysses Grant for the North, went through the tragic formalities of offering and accepting the surrender of the Southern forces.

President Lincoln had succeeded in holding the Union together in its hour of agony. Two years earlier, in an addressed delivered among the soldiers' graves at Gettysburg, he spoke of his dedication: ". . . that this government of the people, by the people, for the people, shall not perish from this earth."

Before the year was out, Lincoln was assassinated in his box at a Washington theatre by John Wilkes Booth, who in his own fanatical way was expressing the spirit of Southern defiance.

Métis hunting the buffalo

In the prairies north of the 49th parallel, now established as the boundary, the wandering Indians and half-breed Métis bands were enjoying the closing years of the buffalo hunt.

To the east, John A. Macdonald for Upper Canada and his colleague George Cartier, representing Lower Canada, were leading negotiations which would culminate in the creation of a Confederation of four colonies—the two Canadas, Nova Scotia, and New Brunswick. Fearing that the well-trained, battle-hardened Northern army in the United States might turn north and quickly swamp separate colonies, Macdonald wanted to draw them together.

The creation of Canada was only two years away, but it was much too early for the concept of Canadian citizenship. Macdonald was simply hoping the colonies would remain within the British Empire. Any thought of including western 'provinces' had to await the building of a railway to the Pacific.

In the spring of that same year of 1865, in the far-off colony of British Columbia, a little cavalcade was meandering its way along the banks of the Similkameen River, blissfully unconcerned with the dramatic events unfolding thousands of miles to the east. The pack animals carried surveying instruments and supplies for Edgar Dewdney, a young English engineer and surveyor recently arrived from his home in Devonshire.

Dewdney was following an established trail through the Similkameen and Kettle River valleys to a point where the trail turned south across the newly-established American border to Fort Colville (in what is now the northeastern corner of the State of Washington). There Dewdney planned to contact the fort's factor, Angus Macdonald, who knew the valleys and the mountain passes like the back of his hand. It was also from Fort Colville that Dewdney was to draw supplies and payroll for the labourers he planned to hire for the building of what was to become the Dewdney Trail.

Dewdney's assignment by the Colonial government was to explore and build a pack horse trail of specified width and stated maximum grades. He was to keep north of the border and use the most direct route to reach Wild Horse Creek (near what is now Cranbrook, B.C.), where gold had recently been discovered. It was important that the supplying of the gold fields and the resultant products be kept within British Columbia and not be channeled south into the United States.

Five years earlier, Dewdney had built the first stage of the trail from Hope to Princeton. All that was necessary there was to bring that stretch up to new standards. Beyond where the Similkameen trail turned south across the border, however, a new trail had to be found through the trackless mountains. It would be over towering heights that Dewdney had hardly comprehended when he accepted the contract.

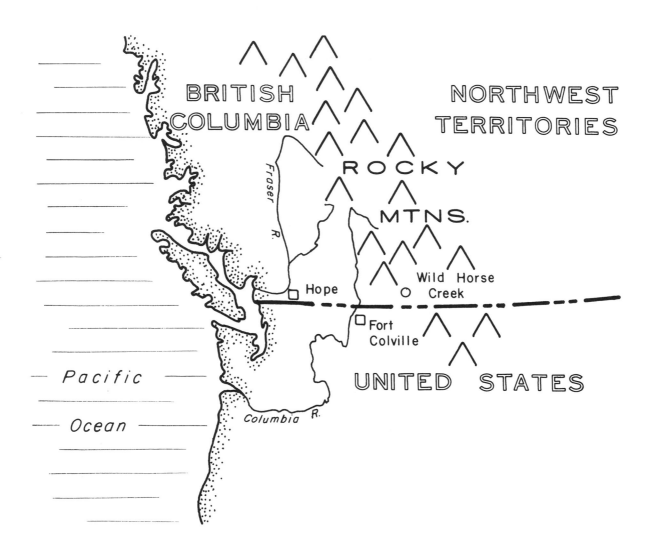

BRITISH
COLUMBIA

NORTHWEST
TERRITORIES

ROCKY

MTNS.

Fraser R.

Hope

Wild Horse
Creek

Fort
Colville

Pacific

Ocean

Columbia R.

UNITED STATES

The wilderness through which the Dewdney Trail was built

As luck would have it, when Dewdney reached the Eholt Summit far above a bend in the Kettle River Valley, he met Macdonald, who was leading a fur brigade from Fort Colville west to the Hudson's Bay Company fort at Hope on the Fraser River.

It was a clear, sunny spring morning when Dewdney told Macdonald of his mission. Macdonald turned to the east and pointed out two snow-capped peaks which he said were some ten miles north of the border. If Dewdney never lost sight of them, however rough the going might be, he was told, they would lead him to Wild Horse Creek. Years later, Dewdney recalled that at first he could hardly see the distant peaks. Then, as his eyes swept the endless ranges of mountains, he finally spotted them on the far horizon. It was only at that moment—at 11 a.m. on May 4th, 1865—that the magnitude of his task hit him.

67

Imagine the thoughts of a young man from the friendly, rolling hills and moorlands of Devonshire, gazing at the awesome heights through which he had contracted to build a trail. The distance alone was intimidating—over 400 miles. Furthermore, he had to have it in operation in one summer!

It would have been quite understandable if Dewdney had shaken his head and turned back toward the coast, where some less demanding opportunity would, no doubt, have presented itself. But, bolstered by an immigrant's stubborn determination not to quit or fail, he pushed on.

After many mistakes, hardships, dangers and difficulties, the trail was built before the snow settled in. This almost unbelievable achievement was in no way belittled by the fact that the gold diggings at Wild Horse Creek soon fizzled out and, as a result, the Dewdney Trail fell into disrepair. But, over the years, the route that Dewdney explored eventually became—and still is—the southern highway route through the mountains.

Later in his career, Dewdney was appointed Governor of the North West Territories, which in those days included the present provinces of Saskatchewan and Alberta. He selected the site for the capital city on the Wascana Creek, at a place that rejoiced in the name 'Pile of Bones'. The prospective city was named Regina to honour Queen Victoria.

A great deal of money was made by speculating syndicates which bought up land parcels along the probable route of the Canadian Pacific Railway. Dewdney was criticized for participating in some of these syndicates, and it is quite possible that he profited personally as a result of his knowledge and influence.

One of Dewdney's harsher duties as Governor was to sign the death warrant of the rebel Louis Riel. Riel was hanged in Regina in 1885 for leading the second of two rebellions by the Métis people.

Having endured the extremes of climate and the rigours of prairie life, Edgar Dewdney was to finish his days in the relatively balmy and peaceful atmosphere of Victoria. He became Lieutenant-Governor of the newly-established Province of British Columbia, following its entry into Canadian Confederation.

Lieutenant-Governor of British Columbia, Edgar Dewdney

The youthful surveyor from Devonshire had become a distinguished citizen of the young country of Canada. And the turning point of Edgar Dewdney's career may well have been on the trail at the Eholt Summit at 11 a.m. on that sunny day of May 4th, 1865.

North West Mounted Police
OUTRIDER

The young 'Outrider' was apprehensive. This was his first assignment as a scout—riding out into no-man's land. Galloping forward to the left flank of the scarlet-coated North West Mounted Police column, always ready for the crack of an unseen rifle, he was checking out a gully for a place where the guns and wagons could cross.

At a possible ford, he clattered through the mud in high spirits—here was the spot and his watch was nearly over!

North West Mounted Police 'Outrider'

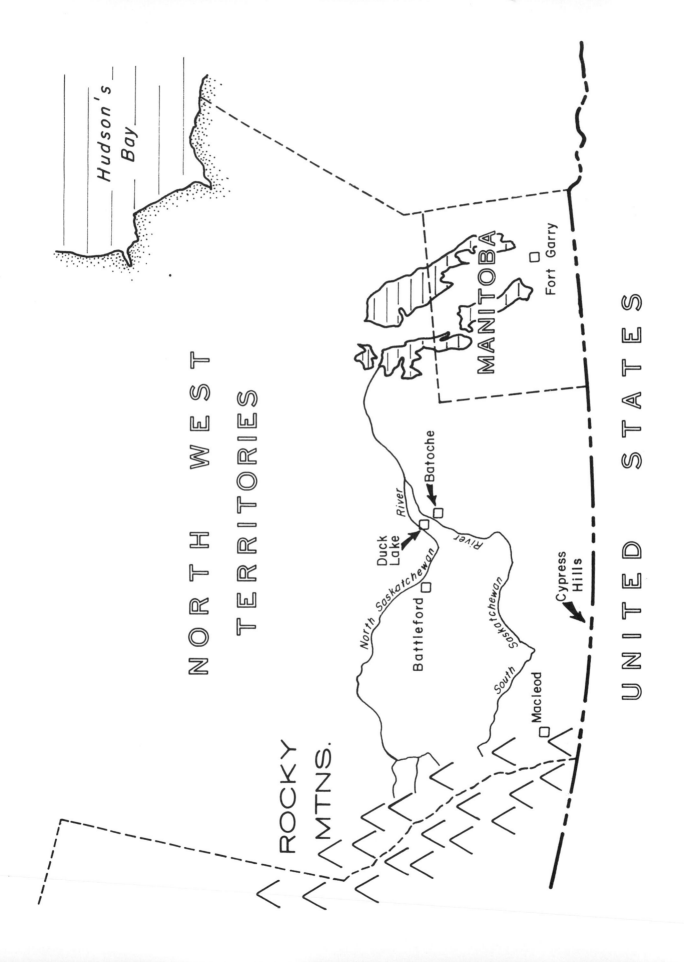

As the sun dropped lower in the sky toward the mountains nearly 1,000 miles to the west, a lone Outrider of the North West Mounted Police cantered his horse down into a shallow gully looking for a river crossing. Behind him and to his right, almost as far as the eye could see, stretched a column of red-coated mounted policemen, six-horse gun teams, supply wagons, and bringing up the rear, a few drovers herding beef cattle.

An Outrider's duty was to scout ahead and out to the flanks of a column, finding the way, seeking out camp sites, and above all, keeping a wary eye to warn the column of marauding Indians.

Here was the very spearhead of Commissioner George French's 'Great March West' across the desolate prairie from Fort Garry, near today's Winnipeg, to the foothills of the Rocky Mountains.

Lower Fort Garry

The column was four days out from Fort Garry and settling into a daily routine. For the majority, there could be no thought of returning before the icy blasts of winter swept the prairie. A fortified camp would have to be set up close to the mountains. For the Mounted Police force not only had to survive the winter, they also had to deal with the turbulent situation developing among the Indians.

Settlement was moving into the Pacific coast area. East of the Great Lakes, the new Confederation of Canada (then seven years old) was firming up. In between, however, lay the huge central plain. It was fertile

73

but empty, apart from nomadic Indians, Métis half-breeds, a handful of fur traders and abundant wildlife.

South of the U.S. border, settlement had advanced far more rapidly than it had in Canada. The Union Pacific Railroad had been built across the central plain eight years earlier. The U.S. Cavalry had established a series of forts to protect the settlers, and in doing so, they swept the Indians from their tribal hunting grounds.

Traders, adventurers and purveyors of pleasure moved in around the U.S. army posts. The most dangerous were the whiskey traders. These unprincipled, enterprising men made solid profits exchanging skins from the Indians for diluted whiskey, beefed up again with tobacco juice, tabasco or anything that would give the taste of "fire water". (Strange irony that some 50 years later when the U.S. introduced prohibition of all alcoholic beverages, enterprising—and equally lawless—bootleggers from Canada thrived on hoisting hooch south across the border.)

While the fountainhead of this hideous trade was Fort Benton in the Montana territory, outposts had also sprung up north of the border at places that rejoiced in names like Fort Whoop Up, Fort Stand Off and Fort Slide Out. The results of whiskey trading were wild debaucheries, murder, sickness and a general distrust and hatred of the white man.

A number of Indian bands, including the warlike Sioux, were being driven north into Canada. Rivalry developed among the tribes as ancient hunting rights were recontested.

Sir John A. Macdonald

Prime Minister Sir John A. Macdonald was dedicated to building a country which would stretch from coast to coast. He deliberately chose a police force and the red coat and pillbox hat uniform, as a sign to the Indians that this was *not* an army and *not* the dreaded blue uniforms of the U.S. Cavalry. The police force was to keep order in para-military fashion, striving for fair dealing in the administration of justice to all — Indian and white alike.

North West Mounted Police

During the debate and manoeuvering in Ottawa over the bill which would establish the police force, there was considerable opposition to the high cost and apparent hopelessness of sending a little group of policemen into the vast prairie. But the alarming news of the Cypress Hills massacre was enough to speed passage of the bill.

The Cypress Hills, which rise from the baldheaded prairie to heights, in places, of 4,000 feet, lie just north of the U.S. border near what is now the Saskatchewan-Alberta boundary.

The massacre followed some horse stealing by Indians from wolf hunters in Montana. Wolfers were not people who enjoyed the most savoury reputation, but even they wanted no part of Indian horse stealing. The indignant characters concerned rode into Fort Benton to gather up a bunch of the boys. This self-appointed posse then set out on the trail of the horses. (An injustice of the times was that if Indians stole horses or were even suspected of any misdemeanour, punishment was meted out to Indians—but not necessarily to those who had actually committed the crime.)

Across the Canadian border in the Cypress Hills, the desperadoes caught up with an Indian band which was reported to have one of the stolen horses. The Indians were drunk and unprepared for battle. After some yelling and swearing, the shooting began. All of the Indians—men, women and children—were killed, the entire band wiped out.

To handle this potential powder keg, the Canadian government had authorized a force of 150 mounted policemen. They were to cover an area about the size of central Europe. After listening to the supplications of Commissioner French, Parliament decided to double the numbers to 300 officers and men. It was this little force that rode out into the unknown.

Commissioner French's instructions from Ottawa were clear. He was to keep the column north of the trails established by the international team of surveyors who were marking out the U.S./Canada border as far west as the Rocky Mountains. Forts were to be built at suitable intervals and the whiskey traders flushed out. Law and order had to precede the arrival of settlers.

All through the hot summer, the column moved westward. Pasture and water for the animals were constant problems. A detachment was sent to Fort Edmonton. After reaching the Bow River, near what is now Calgary, late in the fall, the march turned south to find Fort Whoop Up. Word of their arrival had gone before them and the fort was deserted. All they could do was pull down the American flag still flying over the stockade.

Lt. Col. MacLeod

Jerry Potts - Guide and Interpreter
to the Mounted Police

The end of the Great March came near the foothills of the Rockies with the building of Fort Macleod—named after French's respected second-in-command on the ride west. One of the first tasks assumed by the N.W.M.P. after they were established at Fort Macleod, was to investigate and track down the culprits in the Cypress Hills massacre. Although the police were not successful in having the guilty men extradited from the U.S. to stand trial in Canada, the investigation demonstrated to the Indians that there was a genuine desire to protect the rights of all.

The vital role played by the North West Mounted Police in western Canada became abundantly clear ten years later when a general uprising of the Plains Indians, so long feared, nearly came about during the North West Rebellion. This small force grew over the years into the Royal Canadian Mounted Police, one of the most celebrated forces in the world, serving Canada from coast to coast.

77

North West Mounted Police, 1874
The Great March West of the N.W.M.P. from Fort Garry, near today's
Winnipeg, to the foothills of the Rocky Mountains

In these days of mechanized equipment and so-called progressive ways, it is heartening to see Canada hewing to some fine traditions. When the Queen or the Governor-General officially opens Parliament, she or he is driven from Government House in an open Landau carriage, escorted by scarlet-coated mounted policemen on superbly trained matching black horses.

Any Canadian fortunate enough to see the Musical Ride of the Royal Canadian Mounted Police in Canada, or at Madison Square Garden in New York, is bound to glow with pride at the perfection of the performance and the magnificence of the spectacle. As the ride leaves the darkened arena in close columns of fours, spotlights pick out the fluttering lance pennants, while the band plays "The Maple Leaf Forever".

It is an unforgettable sight and there riding with them, whether you can see him or not, is the ghost of a young Outrider leading a column into the unknown west at 6 p.m. on June 14th, 1874.

Louis Riel waves his cross.
Sculptor Ralph Sketch is working on the plasticine stage
for the bronze statuette

Louis
RIEL (1844 - 1885)

Moment
Number **8:** Duck Lake, North West Territories
11:45 a.m. on March 26th, 1885

Shots rang out over the lone prairie, bleak under a late March blanket of snow. Among the scrub trees, men jerked back, crying out in agony as blood spurted from their wounds. Many died there in the snowbanks and their bodies were soon frozen.

An unarmed man in buckskin rode a frenzied horse through the ranks, waving a cross tied to a broomstick. Was this Métis leader crazy? Was he a hero?

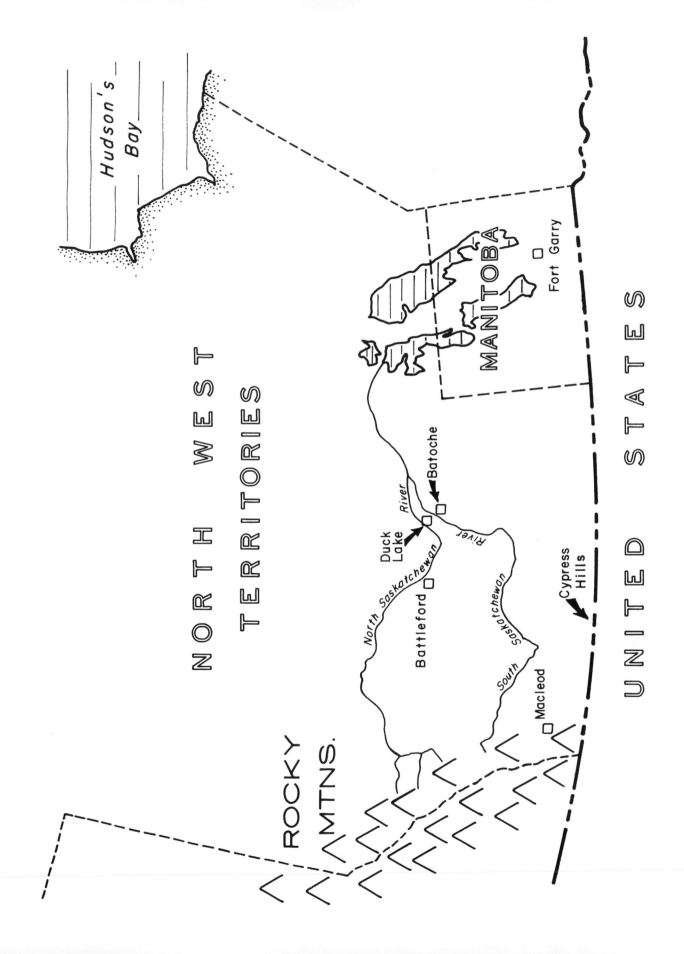

In 1870, the territory that would become Manitoba was in the process of being transferred from the Hudson's Bay Company to the Government of Canada.

The Métis—French-speaking, Roman Catholic descendants of the voyageurs and their Indian wives—felt threatened by the arrival of what seemed to them to be a foreign, Anglo-Saxon, Protestant authority. For nearly 60 years, the Métis had resisted the white, mostly Scottish farmers of the Red River Settlement. Now, Canadian government surveyors were laying out the land for further settlement. The new survey used a pattern already established in Ontario of square townships composed of square sections of prairie.

The Red River carts followed the Métis hunting parties and also transported freight. No iron was used in their construction. Wooden pegs held the frame together and the tires were bound with strips of raw fresh skin of buffalo or cattle. As the skin shrank, it formed a hard, durable rim.

The long, narrow Quebec-style riverfront lots of the Métis were to be taken away from them. With these lots, went their way of life. Their houses had been close together along the banks of the rivers near Fort Garry. This closeness had suited the happy, sociable Métis—they wanted no part of isolation on a large square section of land.

As long-time inhabitants of that part of the world, the Métis felt, quite rightly, that they were being ignored by the new government. Treaties had been made with the Indians, providing them with reserves of land and allowances, but nothing had been done for the half-breeds. No one even bothered to consult them—they were to become part of Canada, like it or not.

Infuriated by this harsh treatment, they chose as their spokesman a young man who had been well-educated in a Catholic seminary in Montreal and whose father had previously spoken out for the Métis people. His name was Louis Riel.

Louis Riel (centre) and his Council, 1870

Riel led his people in what became known as the Red River Rebellion. The Métis succeeded in taking over Fort Garry—stopping the surveyors for the time being—and questioning the authority of the Canadian government. Within a few months, troops were sent from the east and the uprising was put down. Louis Riel was forced into exile in the United States.

Throughout 14 years of exile, Riel lived a lonely, introverted, unhappy life and suffered a period of mental illness. This stocky, handsome young man with a broad face and fiery eyes was, in a sense, a

Bishop Bourget

victim of circumstance. Certainly he had not caused the dissatisfaction among his people—the rebellious mood was already there. For spiritual comfort during the exile, Riel turned to his Roman Catholic faith. A letter from Bishop Bourget of Montreal suggested to Riel that he might well have been chosen by his Maker for some sacred and, as yet, unrevealed mission. Bishop Bourget dreamed of re-establishing the French language and Catholic culture in the Canadian west. He saw in Louis Riel a possible instrument for implementing his goal.

During Riel's exile the Métis were given, as a result of the new government survey, certificates called scrip, which entitled them to exchange their old holdings for newly-surveyed sections of land. In most cases, however, these unhappy, frustrated people sold their scrip at almost any price to middlemen and moved on. They travelled hundreds of miles to the west and resettled near the present city of Prince Albert, Saskatchewan, around the area where the North and South Saskatchewan Rivers meet.

As the Canadian Pacific Railway pushed its way across the prairie, white settlement came with it. Once again, the unfortunate Métis and their frontier way of life were threatened. At the same time, they were faced with the extinction of the buffalo. Then a crop failure in 1884 poured salt into the wounds of discontent.

The Plains Indians were equally disturbed about the disappearance of the buffalo, and became restive on their reserves. The North West Mounted Police had to deal with a series of dangerous incidents—which they faced with patience and bravery. Two influential chiefs—Big Bear, who had never agreed to sign a treaty on behalf of his tribe, and Poundmaker of the Crees—were inciting a general uprising among the Plains Indians, who, at the time, greatly outnumbered white settlers.

A stab of chilling fear went through the white settlements in the summer of 1884, when the settlers heard that Louis Riel had been summoned from Montana to lead the Métis, and possibly the Indians as well.

Riel undoubtedly thought that here, at last, was his divine mission. Protest meetings held during the winter led to the founding of an association called 'L'Union Métisse de St. Joseph'. The society had religious and military overtones, receiving at least moral support from the Catholic Church. At its head was Louis Riel.

Ottawa unwisely ignored the signs of trouble. Suggestions that self-government be granted to the North West Territories were laughed off as unthinkable.

By the spring of 1885, Riel and his military-minded second-in-command, Gabriel Dumont, had decided on direct action — they formed a provisional government. Dumont trained his sharpshooters. The first clash with the Mounted Police came in a snow storm at Duck Lake. Riel, brandishing a gilt cross tied to a broomstick, galloped about on a frenzied horse encouraging his men. It was 11:45 a.m. on March 26, 1885.

Gabriel Dumont quietly and cunningly deployed an ambush. Dead and wounded from both sides fell in the snowbanks; the police, hopelessly outnumbered, were forced to retire. The North West Rebellion had broken out against the Canadian government.

Poundmaker

Big Bear

From their headquarters in Batoche, south of Prince Albert, Riel and Dumont sent out emissaries. They were to enlist the support of Indian tribes such as the Blackfoot — far away in the foothills of the Rockies. Chief Poundmaker's Indians sacked the village of Battleford. At Frog Lake, Indians broke up a Catholic church service and proceeded to massacre the white inhabitants. Bishop Bourget's plans were backfiring!

Only the ever-present Mounted Police and intervention by the trusted missionaries, Father Lacombe and Reverend John MacDougall, delayed a general uprising. It became painfully clear that the rebellion, which was gaining momentum, had to be stopped at once — or tribe after tribe of Indians would be encouraged to join in.

Sir John A. Macdonald, the sage politician, was called "Old Tomorrow" because he often put off making decisions. He could act fast and decisively, however, when he felt the time was right. The new telegraph and the partially-completed Canadian Pacific Railway were to save the day.

The departure of the "Queen's Own" and "Tenth Royals" from Toronto, Ontario. Destination - the North West Rebellion

1 - Scene at the Union Station. 2 - The last kiss. 3 - Shower of bouquets at the Walker House. 4 - Discussing the situation. 5 - Colonels Otter, Miller and Grasset. 6 - Loading baggage cars. 7 - "Goodbye, old fellow!" 8 - Left behind. 9 - The last glimpse.

In short order, 3,000 troops were ready to move from the eastern provinces. Within nine days, they were in Winnipeg after by-passing several sections of uncompleted track on the north shore of Lake Superior. In pre-railroad days, such a transfer of troops would have taken weeks or months.

The 65th Battalion (French Canadians) leaving Bonaventure Station, Montreal

A master stroke of organization had been pulled off by the brilliant, energetic President of the C.P.R. William Van Horne. Suddenly, the value of the railway was apparent to all Canadians. The timing could not have been more favourable; all sources of construction funds—from both private investors and the government—had dried up and the track-laying had all but halted.

By early May, soldiers and Mounted Police under the coordinated command of General Middleton, had broken the back of the rebellion. During three days of attack and artillery fire, the rebels were driven out of their entrenched positions at Batoche. Louis Riel surrendered and was taken to Regina to be tried for treason.

Strangely enough, Riel's second rebellion led to two developments which were far from his objectives. The first was an immediate flow of government funds to ensure the completion of the C.P.R. The last spike was driven at Craigellachie, near Revelstoke, on the Pacific slope of the mountains in November of that critical year of 1885. In the same month, the tragic figure of Louis Riel, still believing in the justice of his cause, walked to the gallows.

The second development was that thereafter, to Quebec, Macdonald's Conservative Party represented 'Les Anglais'. The Conservatives never regained the full confidence of the rural ridings in Quebec. To French Canada, Louis Riel became a martyr—a symbol of the struggle to preserve its language and culture.

Another decisive moment in Canadian history had come at 11:45 a.m. on March 26th, 1885. Louis Riel, astride his frenzied horse, raised his cross, crying in the wilderness to rally his supporters at Duck Lake.

John George "Kootenai" Brown

John George "Kootenai"
BROWN (1839 - 1916)

Moment
Number **9:** Waterton Lakes, Alberta
10:45 a.m. on June 14th, 1895

He had the vision to foresee a national park of rare beauty and a vast haven for wildlife. But the endless waiting for decisions from far-off Ottawa nearly drove him to distraction.

Kootenai was getting old—he feared he'd never live to see the day. But the moment had finally come—bringing with it the joy, the quiet pride of accomplishment.

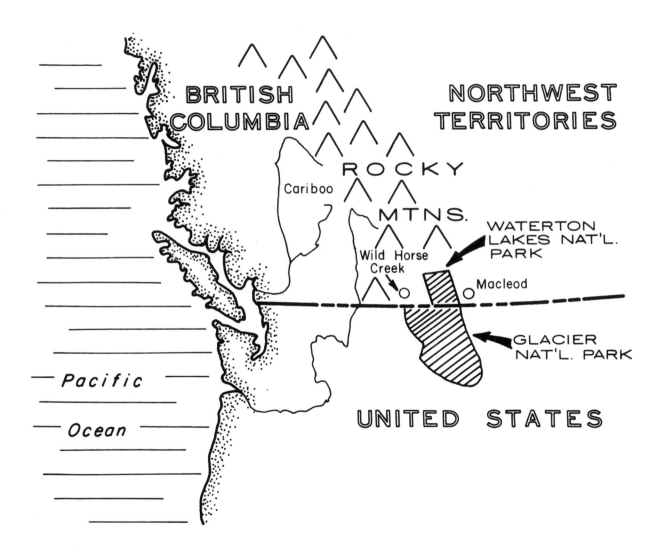

BRITISH COLUMBIA

NORTHWEST TERRITORIES

ROCKY

Cariboo

MTNS.

Wild Horse Creek

WATERTON LAKES NAT'L. PARK

Macleod

GLACIER NAT'L. PARK

UNITED STATES

Pacific

Ocean

In 1839, a boy was born in Ireland who was destined to perform a great service for Canada. He was John George Brown. As a young man, full of the spirit of adventure, he trained to become a professional soldier. Although Brown enjoyed the travel and periods of action, he became frustrated by the British Army's annoying habit of putting officers on half pay whenever there were not enough enemies in the offing.

Hearing that abundant quantities of gold were being found in the Colony of British Columbia, Brown and an army friend, Arthur Vowell, boarded a ship bound for Panama. A short train ride across the Isthmus brought the fortune seekers to the Pacific, where they set sail for Victoria via San Francisco. Like many of the optimists who faced the hardships of the long trek inland to the Cariboo country, Brown found that he couldn't get his piece of the gold action. He returned to Victoria a disappointed man.

By this time, Vowell had had his fill of adventure — he decided to take a safe job in the government service. The ever-hopeful Brown, however, was soon on the trail to another gold rush at Wild Horse Creek. This time he used his army qualifications to get himself a job as a police constable. Once again, the promise of early riches evaporated — even the demand for constables petered out.

After this second setback, a less venturesome soul might have settled for some form of security. But John George Brown was in no way ready for a humdrum life. Riding one horse and leading two pack animals, he headed east in search of the rumoured wealth and adventure of the great plains.

As he rode through the mountain passes, he was traversing the territory of the Kootenay Indians — a name which he was later to take as his own. Emerging from one pass, he looked down on the unforgettable beauty of a chain of lakes nestled between towering mountains. Brown resolved then and there that, if his time ever came to settle down, this would be the place. (Before he did settle down years later, the area was named Waterton Lakes after an eccentric English ornithologist — Charles Waterton.)

Today's aerial view of the magnificent scenery surrounding Waterton Lakes, Alberta

Descending into the eastern foothills of the Rockies, John Brown caught his first glimpse of the vast central plain. Here is his description: "The prairie as far as we could see, east, north, and west, was one living mass of buffalo." That was in 1865. Within 20 years, these enormous herds, on both sides of the border, had been wiped out by wholesale slaughter.

Brown set out on a long ride across the seemingly endless prairie. He followed the South Saskatchewan River, heading for Fort Garry (today's Winnipeg). He wintered at a Métis camp at Duck Lake, where the North West Rebellion was to erupt some 20 years later.

In the spring, Brown was hired to go to the Dakotas as a pony express rider. Little did he suspect why the American recruiting officers had come to Fort Garry. One reason was that in the U.S. it was well known that Indian raids inflicted high casualties among pony express riders!

After surviving this hazardous work, he contracted with the U.S. Army to carry mail between western forts. During one of these rides,

Brown and a companion lost their horses, the mail and all their clothing to a roving band of Sioux Indians. It was only through the intervention of Sitting Bull, the warrior chief who later massacred General Custer and his entire force of U.S. Cavalry at the Little Bighorn, that their lives were spared.

By that time, John Brown had married a beautiful 18-year-old Métis maiden named Olivia. When his service with the U.S. Army ended, the couple moved north to join a band of Métis buffalo hunters. These carefree, friendly people were half-breed descendants of Indians and French voyageurs. Their winter camps were well-ordered and their buffalo hunts disciplined. Brown's account of a hunt vividly describes the mounting excitement.

Once scouts had located the herd, all the riders, up to three hundred in number, would form a long line abreast to give each man an equal chance. *". . . with the captain of the hunt about in the centre of the line and, about three horse-lengths ahead, we would advance at a slow walk toward the buffalo who would huddle together and show signs of alarm and finally break into a fast walk. The leader of the hunt would yell 'TROT!'. About this time, we would be three hundred yards from the herd and shortly break into a slow gallop. The chief hunter would give his final command, 'EQUA, EQUA!', meaning 'NOW, NOW'. Every one of the long line of hunters would spur their runners into a gallop at full speed. From this time on, it was every man for himself."*

Buffalo hunting days.
Drying meat in Camp

95

As part of his varied plainsman's life, Brown spent several years poisoning buffalo carcasses. These were used as bait for wolves which were valued for *their* skins. This somewhat unsavoury occupation came to a sudden halt when Brown killed a man in Montana during an argument. He was imprisoned but eventually released, on a ruling that he had killed in self-defence.

"Kootenai" Brown had his hair cut before this photograph was taken

It was then that he decided to settle down. He took his family—he and Olivia had three children—first to Fort Macleod and then to his longed-for Waterton Lakes. From 1877, Brown spent the rest of his days on the shores of these beautiful lakes. Initially, he was a storekeeper and later he took up homestead land. During the North West Rebellion, he was away for a brief period of service with the Rocky Mountain Rangers, but, for the most part, his life centred around hunting and fishing and occasionally guiding for big game hunters. He also packed supplies in to the North West Mounted Police barracks at Fort Steele, near his old stamping ground at Wild Horse Creek.

In his middle fifties, Kootenai Brown, as he had become known through his long association with the area, was not a large man, but he was a striking character. His buckskin coat, slouched cowboy hat and long, white hair falling below his collar were a familiar sight to the ranchers in the foothills and to the people of Macleod.

Just across the border in northern Montana, the United States had set aside Glacier National Park, which took in the southern end of the Waterton Lakes. On the Canadian side, the Canadian Pacific Railway had built a southern route through the Crow's Nest Pass to the coal fields. Mining interests, oil prospectors and settlers were moving into the area.

Kootenai's dream was to establish a Canadian wilderness park matching the Glacier reserve. He hoped to preserve the natural beauty and to create a vast tract of land where mountain sheep and goats, bear and elk could roam unmolested, unimpressed by an international boundary. His concept was supported by many friends and by William Pearce of the Department of the Interior, stationed at Calgary.

On May 30th, 1895, the Honourable T. M. Daly, Minister for the Interior at Ottawa, approved the establishment of a Forest Park at Waterton Lakes. The park was small at first, but before Kootenai Brown died, it covered more than 400 square miles. Together with the 1,400 square miles of Glacier National Park, it created one of the largest game reserves on the continent.

Kootenai Brown was a man of vision, who, like most of us, had his share of faults. In the course of withstanding sub-zero blizzards and participating in the wild, dangerous thrills of the buffalo hunt, he had indulged in drinking bouts and carousing dances in the Métis camps. He had killed in anger. And he did not promote the ideal of a national park without at least one element of self-interest. After the park was approved, he became its first Ranger.

Generations of future Canadians, as they travel the trails and gaze on the breathtaking beauty of the lakes, will have reason to be grateful to this soldier, prospector, buffalo hunter, naturalist and dreamer, who died in his cabin by the Waterton Lakes in 1916.

Kootenai Brown's most satisfying moment was perhaps at 10:45 a.m. on the sunny morning of June 14, 1895 — he had just received word from Ottawa that the creation of the park had been approved. From a knoll above his beloved lake, he looked at the familiar landscape — confident in the knowledge that the wildlife he had helped to preserve over the years would have an enduring sanctuary within a continually changing Canadian scene.

Washington Grimmer (1852 - 1930)
CANADIAN PIONEER

Moment
Number **10:** Pender Island, British Columbia
9:00 p.m. on June 5th, 1900

The harness creaked; the pungent smell of horse sweat was familiar. Prince, the plow horse, needed no guiding hand from Washington Grimmer as each ponderous hoof plunked homeward on the dusty path.

Washington Grimmer was tired, but his mind was active. He thought of steaming venison stew. He also thought of Thomas Gray's well-known words:

> 'Far from the madding crowd's ignoble strife,
> Their sober wishes never learned to stray.
> Along the cool sequestered vale of life,
> They kept the noiseless tenor of their way.'

'CANADIAN PIONEER'

WASHINGTON GRIMMER TOOK UP THIS LAND IN 1882 AND CLEARED THE VIRGIN FOREST.

HERE HE RAISED A FAMILY, HELPED START A SCHOOL AND OPENED A POST OFFICE. IN THE EARLY YEARS HIS ONLY CONTACT WITH THE OUTSIDE WORLD WAS BY ROWBOAT.

B.C. HISTORICAL SOCIETY   RALPH SKETCH = SCULPTOR
1977

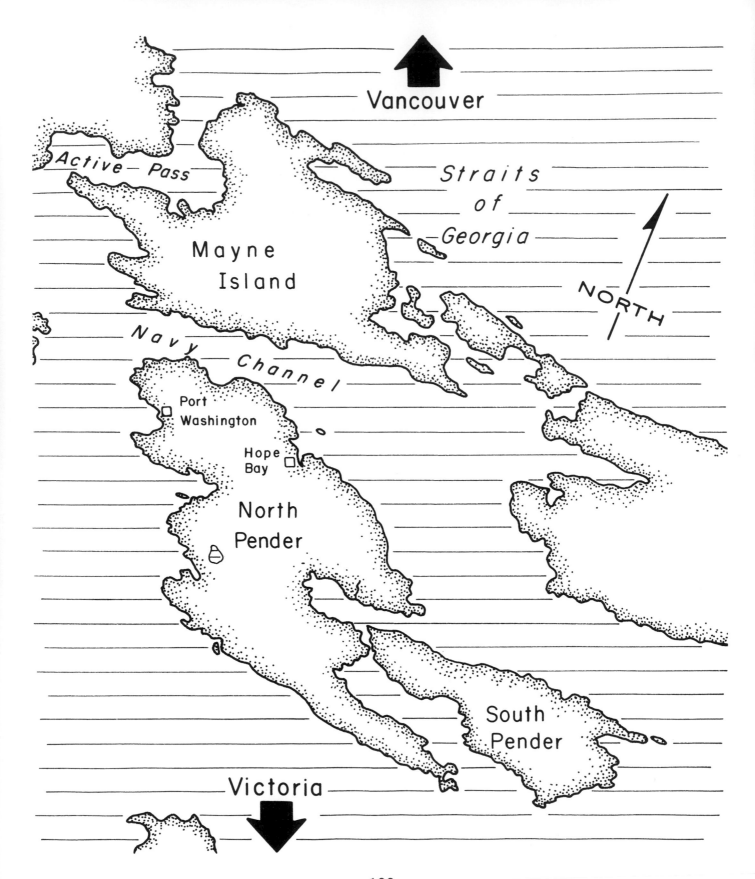

$\mathcal{T}$his is the story of one particular pioneer, but he represents all those courageous people who were among the first to open up different parts of Canada. These pioneers cleared the land for agriculture; they built houses, schools, churches and stores—all the facilities we now take for granted—where there had been nothing but wilderness. They followed the explorers, soldiers and early administrators, but their role was no less demanding or creative.

Many of the pioneers of eastern Canada have been dead for two centuries and some of their descendants are now tenth-generation Canadians. But on Canada's Pacific coast, particularly on some of the smaller islands, the first white settlers are remembered vividly by their children, still alive in the 1980's.

Washington Grimmer was one such pioneer. His father, James Grimmer, was an Englishman who, as a young man, spent several years in the United States. Impressed by all he saw—especially the city of Washington—James Grimmer returned to England. When his son was born in 1851, he was named Washington Grimmer. This name was to travel around the world and find its way onto Canadian maps and navigational charts.

In 1852, James Grimmer emigrated with his family to Australia. The venture was not a success. Among other disasters, their farm house and all their possessions burned to the ground. The Grimmer family sailed for San Francisco and from there to British Columbia. In 1882, Washington and his brother Oliver took up 1,400 acres of land on the northwest corner of Pender Island, which lies between Vancouver, on the mainland, and Victoria, on Vancouver Island.

Clearing the land

Splitting logs

The property was heavily forested. It included good soil in two valleys, along with miles of ocean frontage, beaches and rocky points. There were few people on either North Pender or neighbouring South Pender Island, no public roads and no docking facilities. Horses and cattle had to be persuaded to jump off barges into the sea; then they had to be convinced of the soundness of swimming ashore instead of trying to return whence they came.

For immediate survival, there were plenty of deer, grouse and pheasant on the islands, and the ocean teemed with salmon, snapper, sole and codfish.

The real trials came from clearing the valleys. With little demand for wood products, great Douglas firs and cedars—sometimes 20 or more feet around the base—had to be felled and burned. Some cedars were sold to Japanese contractors who split them into roof shingles and shipped them off the island by scow. Only then did the backbreaking job of removing the stumps begin. Oliver soon gave up, selling out his interest to Washington, who battled on alone.

Pulling stumps

Today's island residents enjoy car ferries, telephones, radio and television. They have neighbours and the use of modern machinery. Washington Grimmer had none of these things. A lonely bachelor, armed solely with dogged determination, he spent years pulling stumps, with only a horse to help him. To get his mail be rowed six miles to Active Pass, where every two weeks a steamer stopped on its way to Victoria. Mail bags were dropped from the steamer's deck into Washington's little boat.

The same row boat took him 12 miles to Sidney, north of Victoria, sometimes through menacing waves whipped up by the southeast wind. There he bought things he could not produce himself. One of his purchases was writing paper as Washington kept a meticulous journal. When his supply of paper ran out, he turned the paper sideways and wrote across his previous entries.

The Auchterlonies, a family from Scotland, had arrived on Pender Island at about the same time as Washington Grimmer. They settled on a large tract of land at Hope Bay, some miles from the Grimmer homestead. After meeting their thirteen-year-old daughter, Elizabeth — fresh from the Scottish highlands, with apple cheeks and dancing eyes — Washington made this entry in his journal:

"I had gone to help get in the hay, my first impressions of my sweet young neighbor, as she busily racked up hay and helped around the home, was very favorable indeed, in fact I felt elated that they spoke so favorably at their resolve to become permanent settlers on Pender. I seemed to have a premonition that this only daughter would become a good friend and companion on this lonely island, although our years were wide apart, she only turned 13 in February and I, 31 years of age on April 24th, 1882, so it did not much look like our friendship would lead ultimately to matrimony, but after 3 years it did, I am thankful to say. This old world of ours is certainly run by a 'Divine Being'. . ."

Raking the hay

In 1885, Washington and Elizabeth were married. A daughter, the first white woman born on Pender, arrived two years later. Then, in the early spring of 1889, Elizabeth was expecting her second child. On a cold blustery night in April, she realized that the baby was coming far sooner than she had anticipated. No medical help was to be had on Pender Island, but there was a midwife on Mayne Island across Navy Channel. The only way to get there was along a trail through the bush to Hope Bay, where a rowboat was tied up.

In a frenzy, Washington hitched his horse to a stoneboat skid, making it as comfortable as possible for Elizabeth with a bedding of hay. The horse plodded his way through the dark forest over the bumpy trail. To Washington, walking at the horse's head, the minutes seemed like hours. By the time they reached Hope Bay, the southeaster was blowing so hard, it was questionable whether they should put to sea at all. But there seemed to be no alternative.

With Elizabeth moaning in the stern seat, Washington grabbed the oars and struck out for Mayne Island. On that black night he couldn't even see the outline of Mayne, three miles across storm-tossed Navy Channel.

The bouncing of the stoneboat and the plunging of the dinghy had a predictable effect. The baby was born as Elizabeth slid from her seat onto the floorboards. To keep the boat's bow into the storm and save their lives, Washington could do nothing but pull on the oars. The baby born in the rowboat was christened Neptune Navy Grimmer. Seventy years later, Nep Grimmer was still farming the land his father had cleared.

As their family grew, the Grimmers helped to start a school. Washington was also a prime mover in establishing an Anglican church. In 1891, he persuaded the federal government to build a dock near the Post Office he had opened. On the first day that the steam ferry called at the new dock, the captain asked the name of the bay, so that he could make an entry in his log. When he was told the new dock had no name, the captain recorded — Port Washington.

Elizabeth and Washington Grimmer in later years

In the lifetime of one man and largely through his enterprise and hard work, the virgin forest and the isolation yielded to most of the amenities available on the mainland. Washington Grimmer was a small wiry man, whose determination showed in the way he pushed his shoulders and chin forward. Old tales of feuds testify to a strong character. It is fitting that his name lives on to mark the village and the bay where the two beautiful valleys he cleared reach the sea.

On a portion of one of the valleys there are now the green rolling fairways of a golf course. Almost opposite the little clubhouse the gate of the Grimmer farm once stood. Close by is a statuette which depicts our final moment.

As the light fades at 9 p.m. on June 5th, 1900, Washington Grimmer, dead tired after a day of stump-pulling, wearily rides his horse home — wondering about his own future and the future of Canada in a new century.

EPILOGUE

Dr. James L. Hughes, educator, speaking at the Brock Memorial centennial celebrations at Queenston, October 12, 1912 . . .

"Whatever else we may neglect in the training of the young, I trust we shall never fail to fill their hearts with profound reverence for the men and women of the past to whom we owe so much."

INDEX

PHOTOGRAPHIC CREDITS

Canadian Govt. Office of Tourism, Ottawa, page 2; **Andrew Niemann,** pages 15, 36, 45, 63, 90, 99; **Public Archives of Canada, Ottawa,** pages 19, 28, 75, 77, 84, 85, 86; **Niagara Parks Commission,** page 30; **Upper Canada Village - St. Lawrence Parks Commission,** pages 33, 41; **Victoria City Archives,** page 57; **Wayne McCall,** page 60; **Province of B.C. Archives,** pages 67, 69 top; **Ian McKain,** page 71; **Carling O'Keefe Breweries of Canada Ltd., Calgary,** page 78; **Victoria Times,** page 80; **Provincial Archives of Manitoba,** pages 87, 88; **Travel Alberta,** page 94; **Glenbow-Alberta Institute Archives,** page 96; **The Grimmer Family,** pages 104, 106.

Author Marian Ogden Sketch worked as a cub reporter in Lindsay, Ontario, and later became a staff writer for *The Financial Post* in Toronto.

In 1967, she moved with her husband and two sons to Pender Island, British Columbia.

She is a graduate of Smith College in Massachusetts.

Sculptor Ralph Mackern Sketch attended boarding school in England and at the age of 17 came to Canada to study at McGill University.

He served overseas with the Royal Canadian Artillery in World War II, and, thereafter, during a business career, continued his training and interest in sculpture.